LEONARDO
DA VINCI

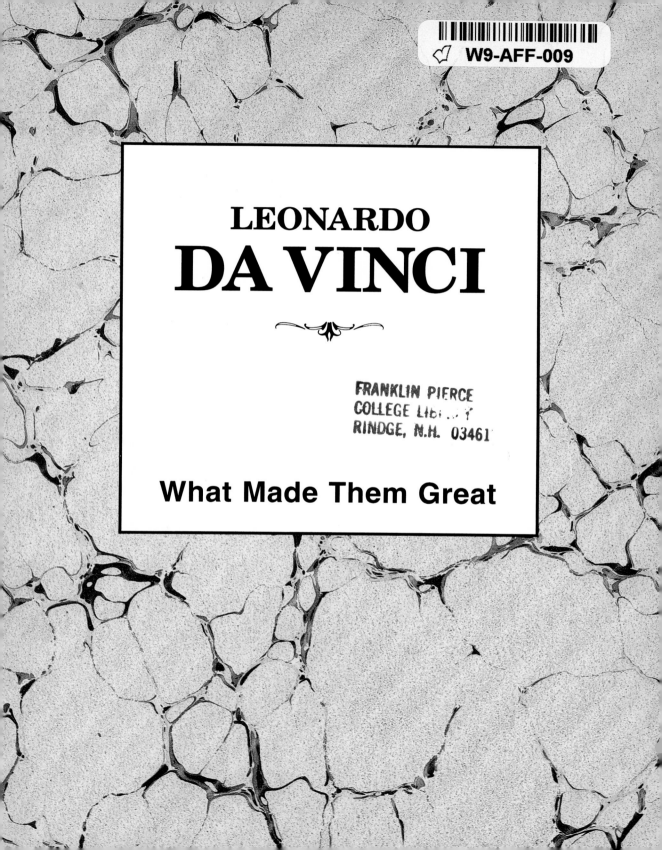

What Made Them Great

ACKNOWLEDGMENTS

Project Editor: Emily Easton (Silver Burdett Press)

Adapted and reformatted from the original by
Kirchoff/Wohlberg, Inc.

Project Director: John R. Whitman
Graphics Coordinator: Jessica A. Kirchoff
Production Coordinator: Marianne Hile

Library of Congress Cataloging-in-Publication Data

Marshall, Norman V.,
    Leonardo da Vinci/Norman V. Marshall; illustrated by Aldo Ripamonti.
    p. cm.—[FROM SERIES: What Made Them Great]

Adaptation of: Perché Sono Diventati Famosi, Leonardo; translated by Ralph Tachuk.
    [FROM SERIES: Why They Became Famous]
    Includes bibliographical references.
Summary: A biography of the fifteenth-century genius, from his childhood to his death.
    1. Leonardo, da Vinci, 1452-1519—Juvenile literature. 2. Artists—Italy—Biography—Juvenile
    literature. [1. Leonardo da Vinci, 1452-1519. 2. Artists.] I. Ripamonti, Aldo, ill. II. Vicini Marri,
    Noemi. Perché Sono Diventati Famosi, Leonardo. III. Title. IV. Series.

N6923.L33M36 1990   709′.2—dc20   [B]   [92]   89-77112   CIP   AC

© Fabbri Editori S.p.A., Milan 1982
© 1995 RCS Libri & Grandi Opere S.p.A., Milano
Translated into English by Stephen Thorne for Silver Burdett Press
from Perché Sono Diventati Famosi: Magellano
First published in Italy in 1982 by Fabbri Editori S.p.A., Milan

10 9 8 7 6 5 4 3 2 1 (Library Binding)
10 9 8 7 6 5 4 3 2   (Softcover)

ISBN 0-382-09982-6 (Library Binding)
ISBN 0-382-24007-3 (Softcover)

LEONARDO
DA VINCI

What Made Them Great

Norman V. Marshall

Illustrated by Aldo Ripamonti

SILVER BURDETT PRESS

TABLE OF CONTENTS

Caterina's Smile

He left Florence, Italy, at dawn, riding alone. The city was still bathed in morning mist. The road curved alongside the olive-green water of the Arno River. The man rode slowly, gazing from side to side. He did not seem to be in a hurry.

The rider's eyes were set deep under heavy brows. On his head, he wore a velvet hat. From under its brim streamed locks of long hair, almost white. At first glance, people could see that he was no longer young. In fact, he was elderly. And yet, there was something extremely youthful about him, too. Perhaps it was his manner, so quick and lively.

On this particular morning, he was moving along with the haste of a turtle. But it certainly was not his age that made him take his time.

As he rode, he kept busy. His eyes swept from left to right, missing little. To his right flowed the Arno River. He could make out fishermen dangling their lines on the far bank. On the other side of the road were trees and fields. Above him sloped the Tuscan hills, all wreathed in sunlight now. He saw a rabbit flash into the woods, the slow drift of the clouds, the wine-red roofs of the houses.

From time to time, he stopped. He would stare at a field or a house, but not because it was new to him. Rather, the sight was old and familiar, something he had loved for many years. Then, he would set off again.

At the town of Empoli, he took the road leading to Pisa. There, he left the main road. He followed a path that twisted up into the hills. The horse's steps did not not hesitate for a moment. It was clear that the man knew exactly where he was going.

In the afternoon, the sun began to lose its heat. Shadows appeared. The colors of the countryside began to grow soft and fuzzy. The rider picked up his pace. In the distance were signs of a village.

Soon, the man was riding down the main street of Vinci. The cottages were humble. Outlined against the sky stood a castle belonging to the counts of Guidi. Its towers were crumbling.

The traveler made his way to a stone house. Around its old wooden door climbed a thicket of rose vines. With a smile on his lips, the man dismounted. As he lifted the iron knocker, a ray of setting sun glinted on the door. There was no answer. The man went on knocking, patiently, for a long time.

Finally, the door opened. A very old man was standing in the doorway. He stared at the visitor. "Have you been knocking long?" the old man asked. "I'm a little slow on my feet. And I'm hard of hearing."

The traveler smiled. It had been a long time. It was plain that the old man did not recognize him. The old man said, "I don't see well. Who are you?"

At last the visitor stretched out his arms. "Uncle Francesco!" he called out. "It's Leonardo."

The old man gave a cry of surprise. "Leonardo! I never thought this day would come. If you only knew how I've longed to see you again." He threw open the door. "Well, come in, my boy."

Leonardo laughed. "I'm 50 years old. That's not exactly a boy, Uncle Francesco."

Francesco was bursting with happiness. His nephew was a famous man. His accomplishments were remarkable. People spoke about him as if he were a wizard. Francesco was curious to know what had brought Leonardo back to Vinci. But good manners came first. The visitor was shown to a seat by the fire. Then Francesco summoned the women of the house to prepare a meal.

At the heavy wooden table, Leonardo sat on a stool. His eyes swept over the furniture. He thought of his great-grandfather. His name was Piero, and he had been a notary. Leonardo's father was called Piero, and he too was a notary. They worked in the legal profession making sure that legal documents and statements were truthful and correct.

As a boy, Leonardo had eaten at this very table. Here, he had spent long hours doodling. Now,

he ran his fingers over the surface of the table,
which was worn and marked by the years. His hands
were interesting. They looked neat and very pale.
His fingers were strong, nimble, and long.

As his uncle stooped to stoke the fire,
Leonardo continued to look around the room.
Everything was darker than he remembered—the
table, the stools and benches, the cupboards. Even
the chimney looked black and chipped.

The old man could not help beaming at
Leonardo. Whenever Francesco broke into laughter,
his face seemed years younger.

"I was supposed to teach you," he said. "But remember how you'd always sneak off? You'd run through the fields to get away. And when I called, you'd pretend not to hear. I could never catch you, you little monkey!" The memory made Francesco chuckle.

Supper was served by two women, who looked after the old man. Living alone, he needed help. They were the wife and daughter of a man hired to work on his land. To the table, the women carried

roasted lamb, salad, and cheese. A pitcher of red wine was drained from a big barrel. The wine was homemade and delicious. It had come from Francesco's own grapes, and the harvest had been especially good last year.

Leonardo helped himself to salad and cheese. But he refused the meat. When his uncle looked puzzled, Leonardo said, "I no longer eat meat. The earth produces so many healthy things to eat. Why kill animals?"

His words made the women roll their eyes. This nephew of Francesco's was very well dressed. But his ideas were certainly odd. He refused meat, just because it meant killing animals!

Francesco changed the subject. Had Leonardo seen his father lately? he wondered.

"I saw him in Florence," Leonardo replied. "But he seemed cold toward me. I can't imagine why. Maybe my brothers speak ill of me. But his health is fine. He's still as quick as a fox."

Francesco nodded. He had a rather low opinion of Leonardo's brothers. All they thought about was money—and how much they would inherit someday. No doubt, they wanted to get their hands on Leonardo's share. The brothers were greedy.

After supper, Leonardo began to explain the reason for his visit. For many years, a man from Tuscany had been working for him. But Tomaso Masini di Peretola had suffered a bad fall. His mind was affected, as a result. Even though Tomaso was better now, he was not completely well.

Unfortunately, Leonardo had to leave Milan and could not continue to care for him. He had a job working as a military engineer, in Romagna. "Who knows when I'll be able to return," he told his uncle.

Francesco tried to guess what Leonardo would be building. "Forts?" he asked. "Bridges? Deadly weapons?" All at once, a thought came to him. His mouth popped open in alarm. "Oh, my," he exclaimed. "You're not working for—" He broke off.

"That's right," Leonardo said. "You guessed."

His new employer was the notorious Cesare Borgia, a warlord famous for his cruelty. Cesare's father was Pope Alexander VI. Now, Leonardo was supposed to strengthen Cesare's lands against attacks from his enemies. In the midst of sieges and battles, Leonardo could not take care of Tomaso.

"Uncle, would you allow Tomaso to live here?"

"Of course," said Francesco. "This is your house, too. I'll look after your friend, out of love for you. But what did I hear you say? Cesare Borgia? Heaven help you!"

Everybody talked about Borgia and his evil deeds. If half of the terrible stories were really true, Borgia would be a wicked man. But, Francesco decided, Leonardo must have his reasons for going. He turned to his nephew. "How did this Tomaso fall on his head?"

Leonardo's face saddened. He had not been present at the accident. If he had been, it would not have happened. "I found him unconscious," he said. "He put on wings and tried to fly off a rooftop."

"Good Lord!" cried Francesco. "I've never heard of such a loony thing. A man with wings. And where did he find these wings?"

Leonardo smiled. His uncle would not have believed the truth.

"You're teasing me, aren't you?" Francesco said. "You always liked to joke."

"I'm not joking, Uncle. It really happened." He added in a soft voice, "But it was too soon. Someday, another chance will come."

The hour was growing late. In the hearth, the embers flaked to ashes. Leonardo climbed the rickety stairs leading up to the sleeping quarters. Nothing seemed to have changed. The smells, the colors, the shadows were still familiar to him.

In the dark, he stretched out on the bed. Every night, he was in the habit of doing exercises in his mind. In this way, he hoped to improve his memory. Sometimes, he thought about what he had studied recently. He would go over these things in his mind, as he was falling asleep.

But tonight, he could not keep his mind on the usual exercises. Being back in the house again had stirred up old memories. The smiling face of a young woman kept appearing.

Finally, he gave up trying to do the exercises. It was no use. The past was too strong. He allowed his thoughts to wander in any direction they liked. As if by magic, the young woman reappeared. A burst of light seemed to fill the dark room. A soft voice broke the silence. His mother spoke to him.

"Leonardo," she said, "off to bed."

Leonardo's strongest memory of his childhood was his mother calling him to bed. And it also happened to be the memory he loved best.

Not much is known about Leonardo's mother. Her name was Caterina, and her family were poor peasants.

In contrast, Leonardo's father, Piero, came from a rich and cultured family.

In April 1452, Caterina gave birth to a son. The beautiful young Caterina was not married to Piero. Indeed, there was no possibility of such a match. They came from different social classes. After the birth of Leonardo, the lives of Caterina and Piero took separate paths. Caterina married a peasant youth, who is said to have tended cows.

Piero also married. His wife, Albiera, came from a noble family. She brought with her, to her new husband, a sizable dowry. She was a very loving woman, and the marriage seems to have been happy.

To Albiera's great disappointment, she had no children. A few years passed. Still, Albiera had no baby. Now, it began to look as if she never would.

In the meantime, there was Leonardo, a bright and handsome child. It was obvious that he was much smarter than other children his age. Piero and his family decided that the boy should come to live on their estate. Everyone loved Leonardo and treated him kindly. Before long, he had become accustomed to his new home, his new family, and his new mother.

The loss of her son must have been very hard for Caterina. However, there was no attempt to keep Leonardo from his real mother. He knew all about the reason his parents were not married. Apparently, he visited his mother regularly.

In some respects, Leonardo found himself with two mothers. He loved both of them very much, although he always had a special feeling for Caterina. Unlike Albiera, she dressed in poor gowns. Her face often wore a sad expression. Tears welled in her eyes. As an adult, he remembered something else about her. She never laughed like everyone else did. Instead, she gave a strange, sweet smile. He felt a secret bond with Caterina.

Growing up, young Leonardo was physically strong and mentally brilliant. He was also very handsome. In addition, he was clever at doing a great many things. For example, he liked to sing. He would play musical instruments that he had made himself. He formed sculptures out of clay. He was always drawing pictures.

When he learned to write, his family realized
that he was left-handed. In those days, people were
superstitious about such things. They thought it was
bad luck. So Leonardo's family tried to force him to
use his right hand.

But Leonardo paid absolutely no attention. "I
do quite well with my left hand," he insisted.

This was true. He wrote and drew amazingly
well with his left hand. He could even play tricks
with his writing. One day, the family noticed that
his writing was backwards. It also was going in the
wrong direction on the paper.

Nobody knew what to make of it. In fact, the
family began to get worried. Perhaps the boy was
doing some kind of black magic. Maybe he was

trying to cast a spell. Who knew what the strange writing really meant?

Leonardo seemed to be amused. "So you want to know what I've written?" he laughed. "Well, hold the paper up to a mirror. You'll read it easily."

"Mirror-writing" seemed unusual for a boy of his age. So did his other pastimes. He spent hours outside, drawing animals. He drew a rabbit that looked so real it seemed about to leap from the paper. He sketched flowers, leaves, and even ordinary stones. Everything around him seemed important and beautiful.

A Break with Tradition

randmother Lucia was very proud of her brilliant grandson. His drawings never ceased to delight her. "Look at this," she said to Leonardo's father. She held up a sketch of a village man. "It's fat Vannozzo Merendone. The nose is made gigantic as a joke. But it looks just like him." The picture made her laugh out loud.

Leonardo's father was amazed. The drawings were done with unusual skill. The boy's eye was sharp. Nothing—not the smallest detail—escaped him.

For many generations, the men in the family had all become notaries. It was a tradition by now. Like his father, Leonardo would enter the legal profession someday, too.

One day, Piero the notary had a startling idea. "Who said that everyone in the family must be a notary?" he asked himself. "What if a boy turns out to have another sort of ability? Why shouldn't the boy be encouraged?"

Piero collected some of his son's drawings. He rolled them up and packed them into a bag. Then he called Leonardo. "We're leaving immediately for Florence," he told him. "Get ready."

A trip to the city always thrilled Leonardo. He loved to sit on the front of his father's horse. It made him feel quite important. The horse was tall. It was fun passing people who were traveling by foot.

In Florence, they visited an artist's workshop. Andrea del Verrocchio was a friend of Piero's. Once, he had been a goldsmith who made jewelry. Now, he did paintings and sculpture.

Verrocchio's workshop made Leonardo's eyes pop. When he looked around, he saw men working at various tasks. Some were drawing enormous sketches. Others were spreading canvases with glue and mixing pigments. Piero left him with a boy who was grinding reddish clay. "Now don't touch anything," Piero warned. He went off to speak with his friend.

Leonardo could scarcely keep still. The workshop was a wonderful place. He wanted to touch everything. He noticed his father talking to Verrocchio. He was showing him Leonardo's sketches. Verrocchio began nodding. When it was time to go, Verrocchio said to Piero, "Bring him back to me in two or three years."

When Leonardo was around twelve, his stepmother became ill. The usual remedies failed. Doctors were called from Florence, but Albiera died.

A great empty space opened around Leonardo. He missed her terribly. He kept to himself, humming tunes that he had learned from Albiera. He made

numerous drawings of women's faces. This attracted his father's attention. "What are you drawing?" he asked. "Is that the Baby Jesus?"

Leonardo's sketches showed Jesus with two mothers. Both of the women were young and very pretty. His father hugged him. He felt pity for Leonardo, whose childhood included the pain of loss.

To lift Leonardo's sadness, Piero decided that a change of scenery might be helpful. It was time to take him to Verrocchio, in Florence. "An expert painter can teach you many things," he explained to his son. "There are rules about proportion and color and shading. You've seen Verrocchio's workshop. He'd be happy to give you lessons."

Leonardo needed no urging. He left the village where he was born and moved to Florence.

Verrocchio's studio was filled with students of all ages. Their greatest desire was to learn. Work had to be done perfectly. In those days, every artist's workshop had its secret techniques. Such secrets could not be found in books. They were passed down from teacher to student.

Leonardo learned a lot at the workshop. He liked living at a boardinghouse in the city. One day, however, that changed. His father moved to Florence and married for a second time. Leonardo's new stepmother was named Francesca Lanfredini. She was young and good-natured, but shy around Leonardo. In some ways, *he* seemed more mature.

Piero and Francesca rented a house near the famous Palazzo Vecchio. Leonardo lived with them. In the summers, the family returned to Vinci for vacations. Piero earned a good living as a notary, but he also loved the land and vineyards he had inherited. Over the years, he continued to make improvements on the estate.

One day, a peasant from Vinci came to see Piero. He was carrying a round cross section of a tree trunk. It looked like a large wheel.

"What's that, Bartolomeo?" asked Piero. "Are you getting ready to compete in the discus throw? Isn't that pretty big for a discus?"

"No, Master Piero," replied the man. "I cut this from my poor diseased fig tree."

Bartolomeo wanted a painting to hang in his cottage. As a favor, he asked Piero to take the wood to Florence. The painter could choose whatever subject he liked. It did not matter to Bartolomeo. Of course, he expected to pay for the painting.

Piero was happy to oblige. After all, Bartolomeo was always helpful whenever they returned to Vinci. Besides, Piero did not have to look very far to find a painter. He had one right in his family.

Piero brought the fig tree trunk to Leonardo. He told him to paint whatever he wished. "However it turns out is all right," Piero said. "Bartolomeo will be happy with anything."

At once, Leonardo got to work. The trunk had been carelessly cut. He straightened the wood and coated its surface with a paste called gesso. When it was smooth, he searched for an interesting subject.

Just the other day, he had been talking with another student about monsters. They had spoken of Medusa, the famous monster in Greek myths. According to the old tales, any person who looked into Medusa's eyes would immediately turn to stone.

Leonardo remembered his father's words. He was to paint anything that pleased him. What he really wanted to paint, he decided, was something like Medusa's head. Whoever looked at it would be horrified, at least for a second.

In a small room of the workshop, Leonardo kept an assortment of creatures. There were lizards, crickets, snakes, grasshoppers, bats, and butterflies. He selected a feature from each one. Putting them altogether and drawing them very large, he managed to create a monster.

For several days, Leonardo labored over the painting. He painted the monster crawling out of a rock. Its mouth squirted poison. Its eyes shot fire. And its nose belched smoke. It was terrifying.

At last, the painting was presented to Piero. Just as Leonardo had hoped, his father stared at the picture in shock. Satisfied, Leonardo immediately lost interest in the work. But Piero knew he couldn't present such a painting to Bartolomeo.

Piero hurried off to purchase
a different painting for Bartolomeo. It
showed a heart pierced by an arrow.
The delighted villager hung it in his
cottage, where it drew admiring glances
for many years.

As for Leonardo's monster, it
found an unexpected home. Piero was a
shrewd businessman. He understood the
worth of his son's picture, which he sold
to a group of merchants for 120 ducats.
The merchants, however, were even
smarter than Piero. They turned
around and sold the painting to
the Duke of Milan for 300 ducats.

Leonardo had already forgotten
about his monster. For his next project,
he was helping Verrocchio to finish a
large canvas that depicted the baptism
of Christ. He painted a kneeling angel,
whose unearthly beauty stood out
from the rest of the painting.
Everyone in the workshop crowded
around. They stared in wonder.
Leonardo was only a boy. But his
work outshone his teacher's.
There was no doubt that they
stood in the presence of a genius.

The Conspiracy

Years later, Leonardo wrote, "The student who doesn't outdo his teacher is a failure." Perhaps he was thinking of Andrea del Verrocchio when he penned those words.

The painting, called *Baptism of Christ*, had stunned Verrocchio and the other established artists who had worked on it. It was an important project for the workshop. Leonardo had been entrusted with only a single figure.

A number of important artists were working there at the same time as Leonardo. They included such notable young painters as Sandro Botticelli and Pietro Perugino. But Leonardo was the youngest of all.

During his years with Verrocchio, Leonardo's skill continued to grow. By the time he was twenty, he was already listed in the Florentine Painters' Guild. This was an important achievement. It meant that even though he remained at the workshop, he could work on paintings of his own.

During this period, the lord of Florence was Lorenzo de'Medici. The adoring Florentines gave their young prince a nickname—Lorenzo the

Magnificent. He was only a few years older than Leonardo. Lorenzo loved the company of artists and writers. As a result, many of his favorites were invited to Lorenzo's palace. Though a generous man, he expected something in exchange. From those he befriended, he wanted obedience and a great deal of praise.

It is not surprising that Leonardo was not invited into Lorenzo's special circle. Flattering princes was not in his nature. In fact, the whole idea of it made him feel uncomfortable.

But there was also another reason why he was shut out. He lacked a good education. From ancient times, the arts had been divided into two groups. Subjects such as grammar, geometry, and history were called "liberal arts." No physical work was attached to these subjects. In contrast stood the "mechanical arts," which suggested hard labor, sweat, and exhaustion. Painting and sculpture were considered mechanical arts.

Lorenzo de'Medici's court was filled with so-called "men-of-letters," who had studied liberal arts. They tended to be learned individuals, who usually knew Latin and Greek. Cultured people believed that painters and sculptors should know both liberal and mechanical arts.

Leonardo had never been taught Latin or Greek. And he preferred the mechanical arts. His most intense interest was in the fields of engineering and military design. So despite his great skill as an artist, some people looked down upon him.

In Leonardo's opinion, painting was the noblest of all the arts. For that reason, he believed that it should be included as one of the liberal arts.

At the age of twenty-five, Leonardo finally parted company with Verrocchio. In 1477, he opened his own workshop in Florence. In January of the following year, he received an important commission. He was asked to paint a panel for the altar of the Chapel of the Signoria. On March 16th, he received part of the payment, a deposit of twenty-five gold florins. His future and his career seemed assured.

However, a few days later, Florence was thrown into chaos. A single event paralyzed the city.

The Medicis were admired by many people. But they also had numerous enemies. Some considered them to be ruthless tyrants. Among those who hated the Medicis was a family called Pazzi. In order to rid Florence of the Medicis, the Pazzis organized a conspiracy. They plotted to kill the heads of the Medici family.

In March 1478, the attack took place in the Church of Santa Mario del Fiore. It happened during Mass. By the time it was over, Lorenzo de'Medici's brother, Guiliano, lay dead.

Lorenzo the Magnificent had also been stabbed. Luckily, he had managed to escape, but suffered severe wounds.

The people of Florence could not believe this had happened. They felt outraged. The conspirators had to be devilish. How could anyone be so evil as to commit murder in a church?

But the plot struck other Florentines as being efficient. Where can a prince be taken by surprise, if not in church? To slay a bad ruler, they pointed out, it is necessary to strike when the tyrant is unarmed. And that meant during a religious service. Besides, some recalled, this type of murder had happened in Florence before.

In good time, the conspirators were captured. Harsh punishment was doled out. The assassins suffered cruelly for their crimes. They were tortured and hanged.

On the day of the execution, Florentines turned out in great numbers to watch. Among the spectators was Leonardo. However, it was not ordinary curiosity that drew him there. He did much more than merely stand and observe.

Stationed close to the gallows, Leonardo was hard at work. He began drawing.

People standing nearby were amazed. At first, they could not understand what he was doing. Then they realized that he was drawing. For some reason, it seemed shocking. Wishing to watch a hanging was considered perfectly natural. Many attended such occasions. But recording it on a sheet of paper seemed ghoulish.

Leonardo worked quickly. He ignored the people around him. His eyes were on the body, still twisting in agony. He studied the expression on the hanged man's features. Swiftly, he sketched the death grimace, with all of its horror.

"Look," somebody called out. "He's copying Bandino Baroncelli's expression. Good heavens, that's going too far!"

Leonardo continued to sketch. A crowd gathered to watch. Their comments did not interest him in the slightest. His handsome face looked serious. His eyes were far away, completely absorbed in the task.

Finally, the sketch was done. Then Leonardo turned his attention to the hanged man's clothing. He made a list of everything the corpse was wearing. On the side of the drawing, he jotted down the color of each item of apparel. Only then did he turn away. Without a backward glance, he left the noisy crowd.

Leonardo crossed a small square, where vendors sold their wares. At that very moment, a bird seller came hurrying over. Leaving his birds unattended, he had gone to the hanging. At the market, Leonardo bought a cage full of birds. Abruptly, he flung open the cage. The birds flew off. Then Leonardo returned the cage and walked away without saying a word.

For some time, Leonardo had been thinking of leaving Florence. Perhaps he should go to Milan. By now, his stepmother, Francesca, was dead. His father had married again, this time to an unpleasant woman who must have resented Leonardo. After she gave birth to a child, Leonardo felt unwanted in his father's house.

More important, it seemed to him as if he'd done nothing with his life yet. He was almost thirty years old.

The Medicis shunned him. He was thought to be an excellent painter. But many of his ideas were ridiculed. For example, people made fun of his designs for machinery that could tunnel through mountains, drain swamps, and lift heavy weights.

One of his mechanical drawings received much humorous attention. It showed a way to lift off the ground a portion of a church. The design also showed how the building could be set down again elsewhere—without any damage.

People snickered. Why in the world would it ever be necessary to raise aloft a building? The idea seemed awfully silly.

One day, Lorenzo de'Medici called Leonardo to the palace and firmly suggested he leave the city.

The reason behind Lorenzo's order is not clear. Perhaps, he just wanted to get rid of Leonardo. In any case, Lorenzo gave him a letter of introduction to Ludovico Sforza, the Duke of Milan.

Leonardo did not waste time arguing. It was his chance, and he grabbed it.

The Colossus

During Leonardo's time, Italy was not a united country, as it is today. There were five different city-states—the important cities of Florence, Milan, Naples, Rome, and Venice. Each of these city-states was ruled by a single powerful person.

In Florence, the dictator was Lorenzo de'Medici. The ruler in Milan was Ludovico Sforza. Unlike Lorenzo the Magnificent, the Duke of Milan had a great interest in engineering. He especially valued any inventor who could design new weapons. As a result, the Duke appreciated Leonardo.

Leonardo was to spend the next seventeen years in Milan. When he arrived in the city, he was accepted as a talented painter. But things did not turn out as expected. It soon became clear that he would find little work as an artist. Nearly all of the jobs he was offered involved engineering.

At first, however, Leonardo puzzled the court ladies and gentlemen. When he appeared at the Duke's palace, there was a buzz of gossip. In the lush gardens and beneath the stately porticos, ladies-in-waiting whispered about the handsome young stranger. Of course, it was noticed that the Duke treated him with great respect. But *who* exactly was Leonardo?

"He's a painter from Florence," one of the noblemen reported.

"No, he's a musician," another broke in. "I heard him play and sing. He has a lovely voice."

"Nonsense!" a third courtier cried. "He's a military expert. Yesterday, he was showing the Duke some sketches of cannons and crossbows."

Before leaving Florence, Leonardo had sent a letter to the Duke of Milan. He offered his services. There were many helpful things he could do for Milan. For example, he knew how to build new types of bridges. They were light enough so they could be folded up. That meant the bridges could be easily transported from place to place.

Leonardo went on to list other inventions that might be useful in war. He knew a special way to dig underground tunnels. It would allow soldiers to pop up and surprise the enemy. He also described a kind of armored tank. It was a covered wagon, equipped with artillery, that could smash enemy lines.

Leonardo also mentioned that he knew how to play the lyre. This musical instrument produces sweet sounds. His various accomplishments impressed Sforza.

Judging by Leonardo's appearance, people were always surprised at his interest in weapons of war. He was blond and blue-eyed. His body was unusually strong and athletic. His good looks reminded people of a Greek god.

Unfortunately, Leonardo also aroused jealousy. Some disliked him, if only because he had not been born in Milan. He came from a rival city-state. In some respects, the Milanese nobility felt inferior to the Florentines. Even the Duke complained about his own courtiers. He was always criticizing them. He called them backward hicks, who could not even speak proper Italian. Compared to the cultured Florentines, they were nothing but country bumpkins.

Once, the Duke invited a well-known poet from Florence to visit Milan. He asked the poet to give speaking lessons to the members of his court. Naturally, this did not please people. So, when Leonardo first arrived, their initial reaction was to turn up their noses.

But gradually, Leonardo won over Sforza's court. He did it by giving them what they loved most—entertainment. The Milanese nobility adored parties. So Leonardo made sure they got some of the most spectacular parties in history. His skill at inventions was not limited to creating cannons and armored cars.

At the Milanese court lived a dwarf, the Countess Cecilia Gallerani. She was much loved by the Duke and everyone else. Usually, it was the Countess who announced the party. "Ladies and gentlemen," she would call out, "you are all invited to the Tapestry Gallery this evening. Master

Leonardo will tell stories and entertain us with riddles."

"Oh, Master Leonardo is here!" people exclaimed. And a wave of excitement would sweep through the palace. Nobody could plan a party like Leonardo. He did much more than simply tell stories. He created really breathtaking displays, something like a circus. Attending one of his parties was better than watching a play on the stage.

One of the most memorable parties took place on the Feast of Paradise. It featured a mechanical planetarium. There was the solar system, complete with whirling planets and shooting stars. The signs of the zodiac were pictured. A chorus of angels sang delightful music. For a finale, there appeared a child, coated all over with golden paint.

This magnificent spectacle was created and built by Leonardo. It was a sensation. Everything worked mechanically. In modern times, we have movies with special effects. It is no longer unusual. But people in the fifteenth century had never·seen anything like it.

Leonardo's parties became famous throughout Europe. Ambassadors from foreign countries begged to be invited. Afterward—awed—they would write home and describe the sights to their kings. Thanks to Leonardo, the prestige of the Duchy of Milan was greatly increased.

Leonardo enjoyed Milan. The atmosphere was much freer than in Florence. People were more tolerant, and he could express his unusual ideas without fear.

Of course, Leonardo's mind was extraordinary. Rarely in history has there been an individual like him. Among the fields that he studied were drawing and painting, architecture, mechanics, mathematics, engineering, and anatomy. He was continually coming up with new ideas. Some of them—like a flying machine—sounded weird to people living in his century.

The Milanese were tolerant, but even so, they sometimes raised their eyebrows at Leonardo. Once, he got into a terrific argument about the Bible's story of the Flood. Fossils of shellfish and snails had been found in all layers of mountains. This led Leonardo to believe that the crust of the earth had changed greatly over the centuries. Dry land now must have been beneath the sea long ago.

Scientists insisted that the biblical Flood was responsible. Leonardo disagreed, implying that the Bible story was wrong.

In addition, Leonardo's everyday behavior could be surprising. For example, he was fascinated by beautiful people. But he was just as intrigued by ugly people. He would be walking along and notice a person with an unusual face. It was a face he wanted to draw but he had no paper with him. Later, he would spend days hunting for the person all over Milan.

Some of his students had trouble understanding him. He was obviously a genius at painting. But why did he waste his time on inventions? They did not think much of projects to extract chemicals from chicken droppings. Nor did they appreciate the oven he built for smoking meats. To some people, these things seemed just plain silly.

In addition to his inventions, Leonardo kept busy as a painter and sculptor. He opened his own shop. Students helped him work on the paintings.

The year after he arrived in Milan, he received an important job from the Duke. The Duke was a member of a notable family, the Sforzas. Francesco Sforza, the Duke's father, had been the founding father of this great clan. Throughout the land, he was famous as a military hero.

To honor the memory of his father, the Duke asked Leonardo to build a statue of his father on horseback. Of course, nothing ordinary would do. The monument was supposed to glorify the entire Sforza family. So it had to be extraordinary. It had to be mammoth in size, towering over all other statues. The Duke liked the idea of a colossus—a giant man seated on a giant horse.

Leonardo got to work on the project. The statue that he designed was indeed gigantic. The horse alone stood twenty-three feet high. The only trouble was how to build such a huge statue. Leonardo began making calculations. He figured that it would take thirty-two tons of bronze. That was a vast amount of bronze, but Sforza promised to obtain the metal for him.

Leonardo waited for the bronze to arrive. Meanwhile, he began to study the bone structure of human beings and horses. He filled many notebooks with drawings of skeletons.

Leonardo decided that the monument should be cast in a single large piece. This method of building a statue had never been attempted before. So his calculations had to be done with extreme care.

At this time, Leonardo was living at the Corte Vecchia, a castle belonging to Sforza. In the courtyard, Leonardo began to build a model of Duke Francesco on the horse. Of course it was not the real statue, for the model was only made of clay.

Several years went by. Leonardo continued to work on the statue. But he never felt completely satisfied. Many times, he simply started over again.

One of his notebooks has a reference to the statue. Leonardo's tone sounds a bit cranky. "On April 23, 1490," he wrote, "I started this book and started the horse over again." These words were written six years after he first began the job.

After a while, the citizens of Milan grew accustomed to seeing the huge clay model. They watched the giant go through many changes. They began to call it *The Colossus*. Over the years, it became a familiar sight in Milan.

It Is Not Finished Yet

I n Milan was a Dominican monastery called Santa Maria delle Grazia. The monks kept pleading with Leonardo to do a painting for them. But Leonardo could not get around to it. There was never enough time.

He continued to work on *The Colossus*. Meanwhile, the Duke gave him other important jobs. Lately, the Duke of Milan was worried. There were signs that his subjects no longer trusted him. To win their affection, he planned a spectacular event. In the Cathedral rested a holy object. It was a nail, believed to have been one of those used to crucify Christ on the cross. Legend said that St. Ambrose carried this precious nail to Milan.

The Duke decided to change the location of the Holy Nail. Better that it should be placed way up in the Cathedral's highest vault. But how could it be elevated? For advice, he turned to Leonardo. Soon Leonardo was hard at work studying wheels, pulleys, and levers.

At last, the day of the ceremony arrived. People jammed the Cathedral. The choir began to sing. By a system of ropes and pulleys, the Most Holy Nail was hoisted through the air. Clouds of

incense hid the ropes. As if by magic, the nail—in its casket—sailed up and up, all the way to the top of the Cathedral.

Sforza was overjoyed. There was no doubt that Leonardo was a genius. The Duke threw his arms around Leonardo. He called him "my own Archimedes." (Archimedes was a famous Greek mathematician, who lived in ancient times.)

Leonardo felt lucky to be appreciated. Not all city-states treated their artists so kindly. For example, the republic of Venice had given a job to Leonardo's old teacher, Andrea del Verrocchio. He was to erect a statue of a local hero, Captain Bartolomeo Colleoni. And like Leonardo's *Colossus,* the captain was to be seated on a horse.

Verrocchio prepared a model of horse and rider. It was impressive to see, but the Venetians were displeased. At the last minute, they decided that the horse was satisfactory. But the captain would have to be done over. Verrocchio was furious. He smashed the head of the horse. That made the Venetians angry. If they ever got their hands on him, they declared, they would cut off *his* head.

Hearing this nasty threat, Verrocchio replied that he would take care to stay away. After all, he could always repair the statue. But he could never fix his own head, once it had been cut off.

In the end, the Venetians and Verrocchio made up. He returned to Venice to complete the statue. But while he was casting the bronze, he fell ill and died suddenly. He was fifty-three years old.

When the news reached Leonardo, he felt extremely sad. Memories of his youth flooded back. He asked many questions about his teacher's final days. It was curious that his last sculpture should be of a horse.

For many years now, horses had occupied Leonardo's thoughts. No finer subject could be found, he felt. A horse was a splendid animal. It was a symbol of beauty and speed. And its entire life was devoted to serving human beings. Leonardo thought it was odd that both he and his teacher were working on horses. Perhaps it was fate.

After Leonardo's success with raising the Holy Nail, Sforza was overflowing with gratitude. "Master Leonardo," he said , "you've performed a great service. I'll be forever grateful. But now you must do something wonderful for the poor monks at Santa Maria delle Grazia."

It so happened that the church at Santa Maria delle Grazia was the Duke's favorite church. Naturally, he took a great interest in its affairs. The Dominicans were very clear about the type of painting desired. What they wanted was a mural painted on the wall of their dining hall. Furthermore, they had in mind a subject. The mural should depict the last supper of Christ with his apostles.

This time, the monks were not disappointed. Leonardo took the job and began work. Soon, all his attention was concentrated on the monastery. Several years went by. Leonardo worked steadily. But he also worked very, very slowly. As time passed, the monks understood that completion of *The Last Supper* might take longer than they expected.

One morning, the Prior of Santa Maria delle Grazia spotted Leonardo walking through the cloister. He hurried over.

"Master Leonardo," he said, "are you coming from the dining hall?"

"Certainly," answered Leonardo. "I've been working as usual."

The Prior smiled. He knew perfectly well what Leonardo had been doing. All morning, he had been spying on him. From the back of the hall he watched Leonardo standing on the scaffolding. In his hand, he held a brush. He was fiddling with one of the groups of apostles. He brushed in the eye of an apostle. This whole operation on the eye took only two strokes. Or so it appeared to the Prior.

After a while, Leonardo brushed one stroke on a loaf of bread. Finally, the Prior watched as Leonardo climbed down from the scaffolding. Making three brush strokes had taken him about three hours. The Prior could not believe his eyes. For more years than he wanted to count, Leonardo had been

working at this same pace. By now, the Prior was growing very impatient. When would the mural be done? Sometimes, he wondered *if* it would ever be done.

In the cloister, he decided to be firm with Master Leonardo. "You must try to work a little faster, sir," he said. "Or else our wall will never be completed."

Leonardo smiled at the Prior. Then he thought of something funny. He could not help laughing out loud. He had a friend named Perugino, who was also a painter. Perugino was famous for working at top speed. Leonardo decided to tell the Prior about him.

"Father, you would have liked Perugino," Leonardo explained to the the Prior. "He was incredibly fast. Once, while he was at work, he was called to supper. He answered, 'Serve the soup. While it's cooling off, I can paint another saint.' "

Even the Prior had to smile a little at the story of Perugino.

"Everything depends on how one thinks of painting," Leonardo continued. "Is it simply a job that pays money? Or is it an art?"

There was no doubt about the correct answer. Leonardo began to walk away. Over his shoulder, he called, "A real work of art is never finished."

The Prior sighed. "Poor us," he thought. But he had said enough to Leonardo for one day. Of course, it had done no good at all.

The next day, the Prior decided to pay a call on the Duke. The purpose of his visit was to complain about Leonardo.

"Excellency," he began, "our mural is not finished yet. Of course, Leonardo is a great artist. And the mural is unusual and quite marvelous. That cannot be denied."

But Leonardo wasted so much time, the Prior went on to say. And it did not seem to be an accident. He deliberately dawdled. Once, Leonardo had been working on the face of the apostle Peter. Months had been spent looking for a model. And what about the apostle Matthew? That time Leonardo wasted weeks to find the right model.

Now, once again, the work had practically come to a halt. The Prior had no idea what could be holding back Leonardo this time.

Could His Excellency help to hurry things along? the Prior wondered. He felt desperate.

The Duke of Milan promised to pass on the complaints.

Leonardo tried to explain. It was true that he did not appear to be working hard, he told Sforza. But when he wasn't holding a brush, it didn't mean he wasn't working. In his mind, he was thinking about the work-in-progress. Later, he would record his thoughts on the painting with a brush.

He also admitted that he worked slowly. But there was a reason. Many other paintings had been made of the Last Supper. Generally, they pictured the apostles seated in a row. All of them wore the same sweet expressions. Off to one side, by himself, sat Judas, who always looked sour and ugly.

But Leonardo's painting was going to be different. He had selected one particular moment. It was the very instant when Jesus announces, "Verily, I say unto you that one of you shall betray me."

In Leonardo's scene, each of the twelve apostles has a personal reaction to Jesus's words. Some of the men look shocked. Some busily whisper about who the betrayer could be. Others are peering at Jesus, waiting to see if he'll explain his remark. Each individual wears a different facial expression.

Leonardo confessed to the Duke, "The Prior is correct. For the time being I've stopped working."

But that was only because he couldn't decide how to paint the heads of Christ and Judas. Suddenly, Leonardo grinned.

"Maybe I've already found my Judas," he said. "I think I'll use the Prior's face for my inspiration!"

The Duke laughed heartily at the joke. The impatient Dominican happened to be an exceptionally homely man. For many people, his face brought to mind the face of Judas.

The Last Supper was finally completed in 1497. Leonardo's search for the face of Christ never really ended. Although he did paint Christ, the portrait did not satisfy him. That's why he always considered the painting unfinished.

During these years, he worked on other projects. One of the most interesting was a flying machine. At the Corte Vecchia was a vast laboratory. Here he kept all kinds of equipment. He studied astronomy, physics, plants, and fossils. There was a special suit for diving under water. An enormous crystal eye was used to study optics. There was even a skeleton of a horse.

But dearest to Leonardo's heart were his experiments with a flying machine. He was convinced that it was possible for humans to fly. Perhaps the oddest piece of equipment that he built had wings. It looked like a gigantic bat. His assistant, Tomaso, was eager to test the wings. Together, they worked up on the castle's roof. They draped the rooftop with curtains so that nobody could watch them. Unfortunately, Tomaso fell and hurt himself badly.

One day, a visitor arrived at the castle. Leonardo was stunned to realize that the woman was his mother. Ill and alone, Caterina wanted to see her son before she died.

For a few days, Caterina stayed with her son. She seemed surprised at his rich clothing. The laboratory with its strange machines was also startling. She was a country woman, unused to such sights. Perhaps for the first time she realized her son's genius. But perhaps she did not.

Leonardo treated his mother with the greatest affection. His expression was full of tenderness whenever he looked at her. In old age, her face was etched with fatigue. But the smile had not changed. It was just as sweet and beautiful as he remembered.

Soon afterward, Caterina died. Leonardo never talked about his mother's death. But she is mentioned in one of his manuscripts. There is a list of the expenses that he paid for her funeral. It was heartbreaking to realize that he could not help his mother. All he could do was give her a costly burial.

After the death of Caterina, Leonardo began to work on a large drawing. In pencil, he sketched the Virgin Mary and St. Anne with the Christ child. The women were young and looked more like sisters than mother and daughter. Once before, as a child, Leonardo had painted Christ with two mothers.

It took several years for Leonardo to finish the painting. Today, it hangs in the Louvre Museum.

In Milan, Leonardo had achieved great success. Sforza had always treated him kindly. A generous man, he had rewarded Leonardo very handsomely over the years. There had been no lack of money for his experiments. He had assistants to help him in the laboratory. And, recently, the Duke had presented Leonardo with a vineyard.

In 1499, Leonardo's comfortable life came to an abrupt end. War with France broke out. The armies of King Louis XII marched into Milan. The Duke was forced to flee.

Like everyone else in Milan, Leonardo was aware of Sforza's troubles. But Leonardo acted as if politics could not touch him. He found out otherwise. One day, a priest hammered on his door. "Come quickly!" he shouted. "They're destroying *The Colossus.*"

Leonardo rushed to the courtyard. There a crowd of French soldiers was busy with muskets and slingshots and crossbows. They were using *The Colossus* for target practice. A rain of bullets, arrows, and stones smashed into the statue. The clay began to crumble. Soon, the horse lost its head. Then, the rider's head crashed to the ground.

At the age of forty-seven, disgusted, Leonardo decided to leave Milan.

Mona Lisa's Smile

The chill of autumn cloaked Milan. Cold rains slanted down. In the courtyard of Corte Vecchia, *The Colossus* sank into a huge, formless mass of clay. By Christmas, it had turned into mud. Sixteen years of work was gone.

In a notebook, Leonardo recorded the disastrous events of 1499. "The Duke lost control of the state, his riches, and his freedom," he wrote, "and nothing remained in his hands."

The Duke had escaped from Milan, disguised as a monk. But he had been captured, just

the same. King Louis XII took him as prisoner. The Duke was taken to France, where he was thrown into a cage. The cage had been loaded onto a cart. Then, he had been paraded through the streets like a wild animal.

Leonardo threw down his quill pen. The past came rushing back. How long ago seemed the feasts and parties at the Duke's palace. How many years he had labored—and how many works he never completed. Now, it was all over. Everything had come crashing down.

After leaving Milan, Leonardo visited Venice and Mantua. Then, he returned to his home city of Florence and rejoined his family. By now, his father was married to his fourth wife. There were many children. It was hard for Leonardo to consider these youngsters as his brothers and sisters. He was close to fifty now, an age when most men had children and grandchildren.

Leonardo himself had never married. He seemed to have little interest in getting married and raising a family. Though he had loved his mother, Caterina, and his stepmother, Albiera, most women in his life were of interest to him as subjects for his art, rather than as possible wives. For Leonardo, his first commitment was to his work.

A few years later, he would begin working on an unusual portrait. A Florentine merchant named Francesco del Giocondo wanted to have a picture of his wife, Lisa. She was a shy twenty-five-year-old, who did not smile easily.

When Lisa arrived at Leonardo's studio, she looked glum. Leonardo realized that she had a charming smile, although it was seldom seen. He called in several of his students to amuse her. It was Lisa's smile he wanted to capture on canvas.

The result—the *Mona Lisa*—is Leonardo's masterpiece, and one of the most famous paintings in history. It is in the Louvre Museum, in Paris.

After her portrait was finished, Lisa was heard of no more. It is said, she died soon after.

The overthrow of Sforza had stunned Leonardo. But he did not suffer any personal injury. In fact, just the opposite happened. It was true that *The Colossus* had been destroyed. But it was smashed by rowdy soldiers on a spree, not because of any official order given by the French.

Word of Leonardo's genius had traveled across the Alps to France. After King Louis XII's arrival in Milan, he made a special trip to the church of Santa Maria delle Grazia. Having heard so much about *The Last Supper*, he wished to see the mural for himself. Afterward, highly impressed, the king insisted on meeting the artist. Leonardo was invited to court.

Leonardo's audience with King Louis XII was to bring about an important change in his life. In the king's royal party was a young duke, named

Cesare Borgia. At twenty, Cesare was handsome, elegant, and well educated. He was a member of an ambitious Spanish family—the Borgias.

Cesare's father was a powerful figure in the Church. Once a cardinal, he had now become Pope Alexander VI.

Even though he was young, Cesare had already attracted plenty of attention. People agreed he was clever. But rumor said he used violence and terror to get what he wanted. His behavior could be unpredictable. Often, his actions seemed extreme.

While visiting King Louis, Leonardo met Cesare Borgia. Afterward, Leonardo told a friend, "Cesare didn't take his eyes off me the whole time I was talking to the king."

Cesare's eyes struck Leonardo as unusual, because they were able to change so quickly. One minute, they appeared intelligent and kind; but the next moment, his glance would be cold and cruel. His eyes reminded Leonardo of a killer bird.

According to rumors, Cesare Borgia was a man who took pleasure in cruelty. People whispered that he had murdered his own brother. Leonardo had no way of knowing the truth about these stories.

It was clear that Cesare had taken a great interest in Leonardo. He knew all about Leonardo's inventions, and was familiar with even the smallest details. In 1502, Cesare offered Leonardo a job as an engineer. Leonardo decided to accept it.

The Battle

esare Borgia and his army marched into Romagna, a district in northern Italy. The campaign turned out to be brutal and swift. Soon, Romagna fell.

Leonardo hated war. Nevertheless, he worked for Cesare throughout most of 1502. An official document described him as "our beloved engineer and foremost architect." Much of his work involved giving military advice to Cesare.

One of his projects was to build an army barracks to house soldiers. Another was to design a port at Cesenatico. He built a fort at Piombino. He constructed war machinery, and he prepared military maps. There were some nonmilitary jobs—a birdhouse at Urbino, and a tower with a circular staircase.

For his job, Leonardo was required to travel with Cesare's army. In his notebooks, he described the things that he saw. One curious fact stands out. During this period, bloody battles were taking place at Pesaro, Imola, Faenza, Forli, and Urbino. And yet there is no mention of battles.

The things that he did write about have nothing to do with war. Generally, he reports unusual customs or interesting sights. For example, he saw a cleverly designed fountain in Rimini. It "achieves harmony through its various cascades of water," he wrote.

In Cesena, farmers twisted their grapevines into garlands and decorated their crops. The shepherds in Romagna knew of a good way to collect their scattered herds. They dug a huge hole in a hill and placed a horn in the hollow. In this way, the shepherds could produce a tremendously loud noise. Leonardo found all of this simply fascinating.

In his travel notes, Leonardo mentions neither war nor the name of his employer, Cesare Borgia. It almost seems as if he wanted to pretend the bloodshed wasn't happening. It was his habit to ignore unpleasantness. Perhaps, he chose not to see the destruction caused by the Borgia wars.

Being in Cesare Borgia's favor was a big honor for Leonardo. The job brought him money and prestige. It also gave him the chance to actually put some of his ideas and inventions into practice. However, at the end of a year, he left Borgia's employ and returned to Florence. His departure happened suddenly. Nobody is sure exactly why he quit.

Soon after his return to Florence, political upheavals took place. Cesare's father, Pope Alexander VI, died. This event marked the beginning of the end for Cesare. Although Cesare had enemies, some admired him. The famous writer Niccolo Machiavelli believed in his greatness. But Cesare

Borgia's decline was swift, and he was killed four years later.

Back home in Florence, in 1503, Leonardo was hired for an important job. It was decided that it would be nice to have murals on the walls of the city hall in the Palazzo Vecchio. One wall was given to Leonardo. The opposite wall was awarded to the brilliant sculptor and painter Michelangelo.

The subjects of the murals were supposed to be patriotic. Leonardo chose the Battle of Anghiari for his theme. Michelangelo decided to paint a scene from the Battle of Cascina, in which Florence fought Pisa.

Both men began to make sketches. Leonardo's sketch showed the slaughter of soldiers defending a flag. The drawing was very violent.

From the outset, the atmosphere at the Palazzo Vecchio blazed with tension. Leonardo and Michelangelo were rivals. They didn't like each other. Their temperaments could not have been more different. Leonardo was good-natured. He had elegant manners. Michelangelo tended to be short-tempered and somewhat unfriendly. Even their tastes in art clashed. Leonardo preferred painting, while Michelangelo was partial to sculpture.

Before long, a battle was raging between the two artists. Florentines began to place bets, as if the murals were a war or a race.

Around this time, Leonardo wrote an essay that compared painters and sculptors. "The sculptor must cope with a higher level of physical fatigue," he wrote. "The painter copes with a higher level of mental fatigue."

He went on to note that sculpture was an awfully messy job, which requires plenty of sweat. At the end of the day, the studio is filthy. It's powdered with chips of rock and marble dust. And the sculptor also looks a sight. It reminded Leonardo of a baker, who is coated with flour.

What a sloppy job! But think of the painter, who works in complete comfort. Not an ounce of sweat is required to lift a brush. "His studio is clean and filled with beautiful paintings," Leonardo wrote.

All of Florence was chuckling. Somebody asked Michelangelo for his opinion. His reply was sarcastic. "Leonardo sounds just like my housekeeper, who sweeps up the marble chips and dust."

As usual, Leonardo worked slowly. He was constantly stopping to check his work. But he grew impatient. The wall painting required greater speed. He tested new ways of preparing his paints. Then he experimented with novel methods of drying the painting. A fire was lit next to the wall. Suddenly, tragedy struck. The paint began to run down the wall. *The Battle of Anghiari* was ruined.

Not long after, another sad event took place. Leonardo's father died, at the age of eighty. Piero had been married four times. Besides Leonardo, he left a dozen children—ten sons and two daughters. Unfortunately, there was little love lost between these children and Piero's firstborn son. The brothers and sisters tried to stop Leonardo from receiving a share of his father's wealth. They claimed he deserved nothing, because Piero had not been legally married to Caterina.

Several years later, Uncle Francesco died. He left a portion of his estate to Leonardo. But once again, the brothers and sisters objected.

This situation really bothered Leonardo. A proud man, he suffered from being treated unfairly. It was only fair that Uncle Francesco's will should be done. Furthermore, he needed the money to live on. For several years, Leonardo fought to win his inheritance. But he was not successful.

In those days, an artist's livelihood depended on attracting wealthy patrons—princes like Sforza or Cesare Borgia. By 1513, Leonardo had found a new patron. He was Giuliano de' Medici, son of Lorenzo the Magnificent. Young Giuliano took a great liking to Leonardo. A dreamy young man, he developed a passion for magic and the supernatural. He thought that Leonardo was a wizard who knew amazing secrets.

"Master Leonardo," Giuliano said, "someday I'm going to Rome, and I'll take you along."

It was true that Leonardo liked to surprise his guests with mystifying tricks. Once, he attached wings to a green lizard, just to see the shocked expression on people's faces.

But Leonardo did such things mostly to amuse himself. He did not believe in magic. And his so-called tricks were not really tricks at all. Usually, they were based on his scientific experiments.

However, Giuliano de'Medici kept his promise. A few years later, his brother became Pope Leo X. Giuliano, too, won high position in the Church. After he went to Rome, he sent for Leonardo.

Leonardo moved into the Pope's official residence, known as the Vatican. Giuliano made sure that he was given a laboratory. Two German workmen were hired to assist him in the laboratory. Leonardo also was allowed to bring along three students, including a devoted young man named Francesco Melzi.

Moving to Rome seemed like a wonderful opportunity for Leonardo. The most important artists of the day were there. Raphael was working on a tomb, and Michelangelo was decorating the Pope's private rooms. Leonardo hoped to receive a similar job.

Unfortunately, this did not happen. He was only given a few insignificant panels to paint. Even so, he began to have trouble with the two German workmen. They were not only lazy; they were mean. They criticized his inventions. They used his laboratory to open a business of their own, making mirrors. Finally, they complained to Pope Leo, saying that he was using experimental paint. The Pope grew alarmed. He had heard about the disaster

with *The Battle of Anghiari*. "He hasn't even started the painting, and he's already trying to destroy it!"

When this remark got back to Leonardo, he felt hurt. He abandoned the panels. Instead, he spent his time at a local hospital, where he studied the corpses of patients who had recently died. He opened up dozens of bodies and drew the organs.

Pope Leo lost his patience. He forbid Leonardo to go near a dead body.

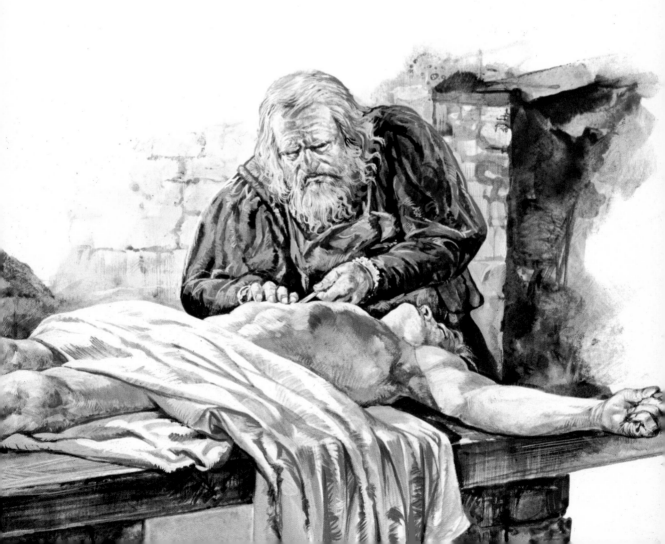

The Final Journey

s Leonardo grew older, he was unhappy and lonely. He fell on hard times. Money became scarce. To his shame, he was forced to borrow from his devoted student, Francesco Melzi. Francesco was happy to help, because he had received an inheritance from his father. But it was humiliating for Leonardo.

During his later years, Leonardo returned to Milan for a while. It had been many years since he had completed *The Last Supper*. Sforza and the monks had celebrated the occasion with a grand ceremony. It seemed as if everyone in the city had showed up to gaze at the marvelous mural.

Leonardo wanted to look at the wall once again. But it was not only curiosity that drew him to Santa Maria delle Grazia. He was worried about the condition of the mural. In painting the wall, he had experimented with new techniques. This made it possible to paint the wall with oil paints. Some people had warned him to be careful. They said that the wall was damp. He might run into trouble.

At the monastery, he slowly made his way to the dining hall. For a long while, he trudged back and forth. His eyes scanned the wall. To his relief, the colors had remained clear. They were just as fresh and bright as the day he applied them.

But he also made a horrible discovery. The wall *was* damp. He looked closely. Slight traces of mold were growing along small cracks in the wall.

Not even twenty years had passed. It was terrible to realize that *The Last Supper* was already starting to suffer damage. Leonardo realized that his work was doomed. In a way, the mural was like a child who comes into the world after a difficult birth—and then dies after all. It was heart-breaking. But there was nothing Leonardo could do about it.

Although seeing the damaged wall was a painful blow, Leonardo took it calmly. He turned away and left the dining hall. Never again did he return to Santa Maria delle Grazia.

In 1516, Leonardo was sixty-four years old. He had become an old man, who looked even older than his age. Very often, he was sick. But his mind remained as sharp as ever. Despite poor health, he was still coming up with new ideas for inventions.

Meanwhile, there had been changes in Europe. Kings died, and others took their places. When King Louis XII of France died, in 1515, the crown passed to his nearest relative.

The new king of France was Francis I, a young man who loved art. Especially, he admired exquisite paintings. He was eager to bring artists to his court. It is not surprising that he wanted to hire the best artists of the day. Apparently, he had his eye on Raphael and Michelangelo. But in those days,

competition for artists could be intense. Alas,
Raphael and Michelangelo were busy in Rome, and
Pope Leo absolutely refused to part with them.

Of course, King Francis was familiar with
Leonardo's work. Who could forget the wonderful
pageants he had arranged in the days of Sforza?
Leonardo's mechanical inventions had never been
surpassed. But the king understood that Leonardo
could provide much more than clever inventions. The
king's main interest in Leonardo was for his artistic
talent. Therefore, Francis set about winning over
Leonardo.

Their first meeting together took place in
the north of Italy. Much time was spent together
talking. It was obvious that the king admired and
respected Leonardo. There was no doubt in
Leonardo's mind that the king was an exceptionally
kind man.

In the end, King Francis made a generous
offer. He invited Leonardo to return to France with
him. Leonardo was promised an income of
seven hundred escudos a year. He also was to
receive a small house in the town of Amboise, in
central France. The king, too, had a residence at
Amboise. There, Leonardo would have the freedom
to do whatever he liked. He could paint, or he could
work on engineering projects.

Leonardo felt fortunate to have a new
patron. Now, he would not be obliged to worry about

money, or to borrow from Francesco Melzi. To show his appreciation, he built a mechanical lion for the king.

The toy lion was awfully cunning. It walked right up to Francis's throne and opened its mouth. Out popped a bunch of lilies, which fell at the king's feet. The lion was supposed to symbolize the king, and the lilies represented the national flower of France.

The day finally arrived when Leonardo crossed the Alps into France. Accompanying him were a servant and Francesco Melzi. It was Francesco who had packed Leonardo's belongings. Boxes containing books had been sent on ahead. There were also his notebooks—writings that now amounted to thousands of pages.

With him, Leonardo took his most precious possessions. Among them was the portrait *Mona Lisa*.

The royal castle of Amboise lay in the heart of France. It towered over the banks of the river Loire. This region happened to be covered by magnificent, deep forests. It was perfect for hunting, which was one of the king's favorite sports. At the foot of the castle had grown up a small town full of cottages and narrow, winding lanes.

A ten-minute ride from the king's own castle was a pleasant house called Cloux. At one time, Cloux had belonged to a high, royal official.

Leonardo's new home turned out to be a very comfortable place.

Not much was expected of Leonardo. His official duties were few. Nobody really bothered him. No doubt, King Francis was hoping that Leonardo would begin painting.

However, Leonardo had hardly settled in when he presented a bold idea to King Francis. Some of the land in the area was swampy, unhealthy, and useless. Why not dig a canal and turn it into fertile land? Think of the food that could be grown. And while they were at it, why not build a channel that would cross through the region of Lyons? It could connect the heartland of France with the Mediterranean Sea, in the south. Then ships could sail right up to the middle of the country.

The scheme sounded fantastic. It took away King Francis's breath. He agreed enthusiastically. Excited, Leonardo got to work studying the terrain and drawing up plans.

But almost immediately, the king's advisers stepped in. They warned the king that Leonardo's idea was too ambitious and too expensive. In the end, the king backed down.

By now, Leonardo realized that no real work would be possible. Nobody took his designs seriously. He was nothing more than an honored guest in France. And so, after that, he stopped trying.

His last painting was of St. John the Baptist. The picture has long mystified viewers, because the figure has some features of a man and others of a woman.

Mostly, Leonardo spent his time with Francesco Melzi at Cloux. Melzi did his best to look after his master and to entertain him.

Leonardo and Melzi would walk in the woods together. When they stopped to rest, Leonardo would sit for hours studying the plants and flowers.

In time, Leonardo made his will. His writings and his art supplies were left to Francesco Melzi. There was no doubt in his mind that the young man would care for them well.

It was springtime at Cloux. By now, Leonardo had grown extremely feeble. One of his hands became crippled. He had trouble holding a brush.

One day, he and Francesco found an injured bird. It was a swallow, too hurt to migrate south with the rest of the flock. Looking for a home, the bird had made a nest inside the house. Leonardo and his student discovered the poor thing under a stairway. Nursed with tender care, the swallow got well. But even after its injuries had healed, the men kept it as a pet.

Finally, Leonardo could no longer rise from his bed. He died on May 2, 1519, at the age of sixty-seven. That day, a weeping Francesco flung

open a window and gave the swallow its freedom. A
moment later, the bird was gone.

Francesco went to see the village priest in
Amboise. "My master died," he announced. "I've
come to arrange for the burial."

Leonardo had left careful instructions. He
was to be buried in the Church of St. Florentine. In
the palace church, more than thirty Masses were to
be celebrated. These services were to be repeated in
all the other churches of Amboise, as well.

Then Francesco returned to Cloux and wrote to Leonardo's family. In spite of their quarrels in the past, they would receive what little money remained in his estate. Everything of importance to Leonardo—his drawings and writings—was left to Francesco.

A few days later, Leonardo was buried. His tomb was placed in the choir of the church.

After death, curious things happened to his casket. About forty years later, the coffins in St. Florentine were wrecked by vandals. The skeletons of the buried were mixed and scattered.

More than two centuries passed. During the French Revolution, the church itself was completely torn down. The stones were hauled away. Caskets were melted down, and the lead was sold. Bones were collected, and placed in a single grave.

During the nineteenth century, a band of scientists came to Amboise. Digging near the place where the church had once stood, they discovered the foundation of a very old building. Under a pile of rubble was found a skeleton and fragments of a tombstone. On one of the pieces were etched the letters LEO. Another read INC. The scholars continued to dig. A third fragment said DUS.

Did these letters once spell LEONARDUS and VINCI? Had this tomb belonged to one of the most brilliant minds in human history? There was just not enough evidence to say for certain.

Leonardo da Vinci's Manuscripts

Most of Leonardo's existing manuscripts come from the compilation that he entrusted to his devoted student, Francesco Melzi, in France, before his death. They are referred to as *codices*. Each codex is designated by letter, to identify it. A few codices are cited below. They are scattered in libraries and museums in Europe. Some are mysterious fragments of works, which in most cases the author probably would have arranged differently from various "compilers."

Codex A—*Written in 1492. Various Subjects. It is now in the Library of the Institut de France, in Paris, where codices through the letter K are located.*

Codex B—*Written in 1498. Subject: Military design.*

Codex C—*Written in 1490. Called the Codex of Light and Shadow, due to its subject.*

Codex D—*Written in 1508. Subject: Optics.*

Codex E—*Written in 1513-1514. Subject: Geometry and the flight of birds.*

Codex F—*Written in 1508-1509. Subject: Hydraulics.*

Codex VU—*Written in 1505. Subject: The flight of birds. It is located in the Royal Library in Turin, Italy.*

Codex ATL—*Written between 1483 and 1518. This is known as the Atlantic Codex. It is in the Ambrosian Library in Milan, Italy.*

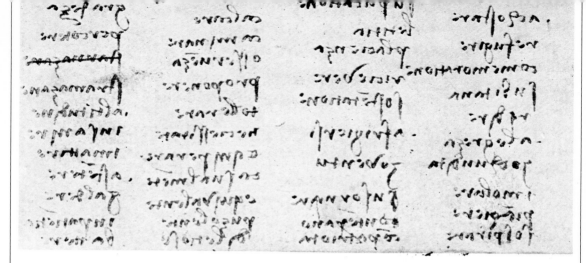

Leonardo manuscript—dealing with the topic of grammar and a Latin-Italian dictionary

Codex TR—*Written in 1498. Subject: Notes and drawings about language. It is located in the Library of the Sforza Castle in Milan, Italy.*

Codex LEI—*(Leicester) Written in 1504-1506. Subject: Hydraulics. It is located in the Victoria and Albert Museum in London, England.*

Windsor Collection—*A collection of drawings and anatomical studies with pages based on two of Leonardo's notebooks. It is located in the Royal Library at Windsor Castle in England.*

Leonardo wrote with his left hand "in reverse," that is, writing letters and words from right to left. Therefore, to read his writing, it's necessary to use a mirror. The work of deciphering the manuscripts has been going on since 1800. In 1902, the da Vinci Commission was created for the in-depth study and clarification of his voluminous scientific and literary works (5,000 pages), which had been almost forgotten for centuries.

Leonardo and Water

The following fragment was taken from the *Atlantic Codex*. (Some words and phrases have been simplified for ease of understanding.)

Among the causes of injury to man and damage to his belongings, it seems to me that rivers, with their sudden floods, are at the top. If one were to place the damage caused by fire before that of violent rivers, I believe he would be in error. Indeed, fire stops and goes out once there's nothing for it to consume, but no human measure is effective against the flooding of swollen and haughty rivers. Flooding with turbulent waves erodes and deepens high banks, destroys lands under cultivation by carrying off topsoil, demolishes houses, and uproots trees and sweeps them off like booty to their resting place in the sea. It takes with it people, plants, and animals alike, and it destroys dikes and other structures. It drags light things along with it and ruins heavy ones, transforming small clefts in the land into great precipices. How important it is to get away from such a neighbor! How many cities, how many fields, castles, towns, and houses have been consumed! How the efforts of farmers vanish! How many families shattered and submerged! All this without mentioning the flocks lost to drowning!

Water undermines mountains and fills valleys. I should like to reduce the earth to a perfect level sphere, if I could.

This fragment makes clear Leonardo's close observation of the phenomenon of floods and the human toll involved. But Leonardo also knew that waters that were so dangerous *un*harnessed could be harnessed and used for irrigation. In his youth, and throughout his life, he conceived ingenious projects to channel and distribute precious water to farmland. Only in Lombardy (Italy) did the lords take advantage of his studies, and the region enjoyed—and enjoys to this day—an irrigation system to make it fertile.

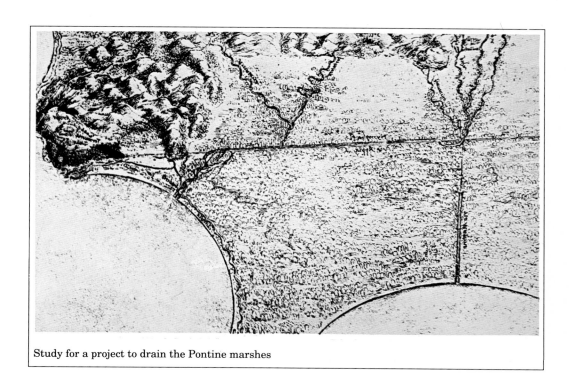

Study for a project to drain the Pontine marshes

Leonardo, Beauty, and Fashion

Leonardo's appearance was elegant, composed, and serious. He always liked to dress well. Moreover, for many years his surroundings were the courts of the nobles. But the excessive luxury, ornament, and eccentricities of fashion bothered him. He never confused them with beauty, and he didn't consider them worth painting. True beauty was elsewhere, in the intensity of expression and the mirror of nature. "Have you never seen women from the hills wrapped in simple, humble materials take on greater beauty than those women in their finery?" (FROM THE *Urbinate Codex* in the Vatican Library)

From notes found in the same codex, we cite his advice to painters, which serves as the pretext for a brilliant satire on useless and capricious fashion.

*A*void, to the extent possible, showing *your painted figures in contemporary dress. More than raising our descendant's admiration for their dignity and beauty, it will give them reason to laugh at man's crazy inventions.*

I don't recall seeing men dressed in fringed (braided, scalloped) outfits all around in my childhood, but when this custom first appeared, it was considered so beautiful that even the fringe was fringed, along with hoods and shoes. . . . Later, I noticed that shoes,

Cecchino da Verona—*Page with Grapes*   Master of the Cape—*Gentleman Joshua*

*berets, belt pouches, arms, necklaces, sleeves
on jerkins, trains on dresses, all came to a
long, narrow point. Then sleeves started to
grow, and grew so large that a single sleeve
was larger than the garment itself; afterward
dresses started to come up around the neck,
so much so that they finally covered the entire
head; then they started to strip them away in
such a way that the material couldn't be held
up by the shoulders, because it didn't rest on
them. Then they started to make clothing
longer, to the point that men constantly had
their arms full of material so they wouldn't
step on it. Then they made clothes narrower
to inflict great torture and many died in them.
People's feet were so squeezed that their toes
ended up one on top of another and became
covered with calluses.*

Observations of Nature

The notes that follow, from *The Treatise on Painting*, refer to botany, which is the study of plant life. But Leonardo intended them for painters, so that they would learn how to depict nature accurately.

Any youngster could verify Leonardo's assertions, draw them, and not forget them, which to Leonardo meant learning them.

Flowers on the Branches of Herbs

Of the flowers that bloom on the branches of herbs, some flowers appear at the end of these branches, while others open their first petal at the bottom end of the stalk.

Branches on Plants

First: On any plant, all branches that are not held down by their own weight curve upward, leading their tips toward the sky.

Second: On trees, the little branches that grow from other branches are bigger, if they grow from under the branch than from the top of the branch.

Third: All little branches that grow in the center of the trees disappear before long, because of excessive shade.

Fourth: Those branches near the top of a tree will be more vigorous, because of the air and sunlight.

Leonardo da Vinci
Study of Flowers

Fifth: The angle at which different branches divide on a tree is the same.

Sixth: But the angle becomes more obtuse as the branches at the sides get older.

*Seventh: The two forks in a branch, taken together, are equal to the diameter of the branch from which they grow. That is (see illustration): **a** and **b** together equal **e**; **c** and **d** together equal **f**; and **f** and **e** together equal the diameter of branch **o p**, which is equal in diameter to **a b c d**. This is so because the fluids in the largest one divide evenly into the branches.*

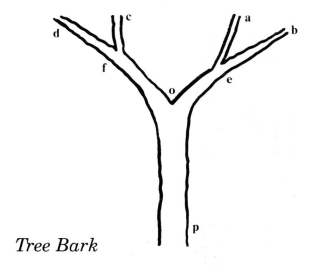

Tree Bark

The tree bark always splits along the length of the tree, except for cherry trees, whose bark splits in circles. The bark on the trunk at the upper part of old trees is always covered with a feathery green moss.

Tree bark always has larger splits in the lower part than in the upper part of the tree.

HISTORICAL CHRONOLOGY

Life of Leonardo da Vinci	Historical and Cultural Events
	1451 Christopher Columbus is born in Genoa.
1452 Leonardo born in Anchiano (township of Vinci). Illegitimate son of Piero, the notary, and Caterina, a young peasant woman.	**1452** Piero della Francesca begins a cycle of frescoes about the legend of the True Cross at San Francesco, in Arezzo.
1453 End of the Hundred Years War and the expulsion of the English from France. Andrea del Verrocchio, eighteen years old, is found innocent of manslaughter for having killed a man while throwing stones.	
1454 The peace of Lodi: a period of peace begins, sustained principally by the Medicis in Florence. The largest states in Italy are the republic of Venice, the duchy of Milan, Florence, the Vatican, and the kingdom of Naples.	

Piero della Francesca—
Dream of Constantine
(Arezzo, San Francesco)

Andrea del
Verrocchio—
*Baptism of
Christ (*Uffizi
Gallery,
Florence,
Italy)

Life of Leonardo da Vinci	Historical and Cultural Events
	1456 Johann Gutenberg invents the printing press, with movable type.
1469 Leonardo is brought to Verrocchio's workshop in Florence, by his father.	**1469** In Toledo, Spain, the marriage of Ferdinand of Aragon and Isabella of Castile signals the beginnings of the Spanish nation.
1472 Leonardo is inscribed into the Florentine Painters Guild.	

Wooden sculpture—*Isabella of Castile* (Cathedral at Granada, Spain)

Gutenberg's Press— *Deuteronomy* (Gutenberg Museum, Mainz, Germany)

Leonardo da Vinci— *Madonna of the Carnation* (Alte Pinakotek, Munich, Germany)

Life of Leonardo da Vinci	Historical and Cultural Events
1478 Leonardo paints his *Annunciation, Madonna of the Carnation,* and *Madonna of the Flower.*	**1478** The conspiracy of the Pazzi. Giuliano de' Medici dies in Santa Maria del Fiore; Lorenzo survives.
1483 Leonardo seeks the support of Ludovico Sforza (the "Duke"), who rules the duchy of Milan, in place of his nephew, Gian Galeazzo.	**1483** The birth of Raphael Sanzio. Martin Luther is born in Eisleben, Germany. Verrocchio executes the *Equestrian Monument of Colleoni,* his masterpiece.
	1485 Hernando Cortés, the future conqueror of Mexico, is born in Extremadura, Spain.
1489 Leonardo paints portraits of Sforza's favorite ladies, Cecilia Gallerani and Lucrecia Crivelli.	

Andrea del Verrocchio—*Monument of Bartolomeo Colleoni* (Venice, Italy)

Life of Leonardo da Vinci	Historical and Cultural Events
1490 The *Feast of Paradise* produced in the Sforza Castle. Scenery and costumes designed by Leonardo.	**1490** The young Albrecht Dürer, who will become the most famous German artist, departs on a study trip to Italy.
1492 Leonardo carries out a study to make navigable the Martesana Canal, from Trezzo to Milan. He paints and decorates the Duke's private rooms.	**1492** Lorenzo the Magnificent dies. The reconquest of Granada by Ferdinand and Isabella. With the fall of its last stronghold the Moorish presence in Spain ends. Queen Isabella finances Columbus's expedition. On October 12, Columbus discovers America.

Leonardo da Vinci—*Lady with an Ermine* (Czartorisky Museum, Krakow, Poland)

Albrecht Dürer—*Self-Portrait* (Prado Museum, Madrid, Spain)

Life of Leonardo da Vinci	Historical and Cultural Events
1496 Leonardo works on *The Last Supper* in the Monastery of Santa Maria delle Grazia, in Milan.	**1496** Columbus returns from his second voyage, still convinced that he reached Asia.
	1498 Michelangelo sculpts the *Pietà*.
1499 Leonardo receives a vineyard from the Duke.	**1499** October—King Louis XII of France enters Milan (Italy).

Ambrogio de Predis—*Ludovico il Moro* (Trivulcian Library, Milan, Italy)

Anonymous—*Portrait of Leonardo da Vinci* (Museum of Science and Technology, Milan, Italy)

Life of Leonardo da Vinci	Historical and Cultural Events
1500 The model of the monument to the Duke's father (called *The Colossus*) is destroyed by French soldiers. Leonardo goes first to Venice and later to Florence. He paints the *Mona Lisa* (*La Gioconda*).	**1500** Sforza, the Duke, is taken prisoner by the French. The first textile mills are built in England.
1502 Leonardo in the service of Duke Valentino (Cesare Borgia, son of Pope Alexander VI) as engineer and architect in Romagna.	
1503 Leonardo is in Florence, among the experts who decide where to place Michelangelo's *David*.	**1503** The challenge of Barletta. Pope Alexander VI dies. Julius II, a Franciscan priest, is chosen as pope.
1507 The French return to Leonardo the vineyard given to him by Sforza. Leonardo undertakes new hydraulic and mechanical engineering projects.	**1507** Cesare Borgia dies in exile, at the age of thirty-six.

Life of Leonardo da Vinci	Historical and Cultural Events
	1508 Sforza, the Duke, dies in prison.
1509 Leonardo constructs the backdrop for the triumphal entrance of King Louis XII into Milan.	**1509** Michelangelo completes the *Story of Noah,* the *Prophets,* and the *Sibyls* for the Sistine Chapel.
1512 Lawsuits brought by Leonardo's siblings over the inheritance from Uncle Francesco continue.	**1512** The armies of the Holy Alliance, at Pope Julius II's insistence, oblige the French to leave Milan.
1513 Leonardo is in Florence. He goes later to Rome, where he attends the coronation of the new pope, Leo X (Giovanni de' Medici, son of Lorenzo the Magnificent).	**1513** Pope Julius II dies. Albrecht Dürer engraves *Horseman, Death, and the Devil,* thus concluding his equestrian studies, which were influenced by Leonardo's preliminary studies for *The Colossus.*
1515 Leonardo is in Bologna on the occasion of the agreement between Francis I of France and Pope Leo X.	**1515** King Francis I succeeds Louis XII as king of France and reconquers the duchy of Milan.

Life of Leonardo da Vinci	Historical and Cultural Events
1516 Leonardo goes to France as painter to King Francis I.	
	1517 The monk Martin Luther publishes his *95 Theses,* questioning papal authority.
1518 Leonardo, ill in Amboise, is cared for by his student, Francesco Melzi.	
1519 Leonardo dies. He leaves his manuscripts to Francesco Melzi.	**1519** Magellan departs to sail around the world. Hernando Cortés conquers Mexico.

Michelangelo—*Delphic Sibyl* (Sistine Chapel, Vatican)

Leonardo da Vinci—*St. John the Baptist* (Louvre Museum, Paris, France)

Leonardo da Vinci— *Virgin and Child with St. Anne* (Louvre Museum)

BOOKS FOR FURTHER READING

Da Vinci by Mike Venezia, Children's Press, 1989.

Leonardo and the Renaissance, Nathaniel Harris, Watts, 1987.

Leonardo da Vinci by Ernest Raboff, Harper Junior Books, 1987.

Leonardo da Vinci: The Artist, Inventor, Scientist in Three-Dimensional Movable Pictures by Alice and Martin Provensen, Viking Kestrel, 1984.

INDEX